Thuribles

Thuribles

Poems by

John Fritzell

Cover design by Shay Culligan

ISBN: 978-1-954353-56-5

Kelsay Books
502 South 1040 East, A-119
American Fork, Utah, 84003

For Mom and Dad

Acknowledgments

I am grateful to the editors of the following publications for first publishing my poems (some in slightly different forms), as noted.

Autumn Sky Poetry Daily: "Paddling with Dragonflies"
Bramble: "A Hymn for Miley"
Canoe & Kayak Magazine: "Down River"
Gray's Sporting Journal: "Epitaph for a Duck Hunter"
Plainsongs: "Last Missile," "To Aunt Sara"
Red Eft Review: "Death of a Naturalist," "Self-Quarantined"
Tiny Seed Literary Journal: "Cattails," "Early Modern Junco"
Wisconsin Fellowship of Poets Poet's Calendar: "Fritillaries"

Contents

Down River

We all start heading down river,
past the two boulders and through the chute,
casting our lines to the deepest pools
and dragging them out across the gravel
like cruising crustacea in flight from smallmouths.

The first fling dangles from a blueberry bush
and comes shooting back across the bow,
another toss is cut short by a timid bail,
but the Rebel finally settles in beyond the shadowed boulder,
arching downstream and tugging into the current.

Such a current, we hope, will last forever,
at least until the roar of Big Quinn Rapids
where the river's swift flow cools
our anxiety that the float will soon end
with nothing in the basket or an empty stringer.

We pass by Bear Skull Rock, knowing only
that The Ledge and the final standing wave await
to wake us up before the flowage,
where all the flowing stops and where all we hear
are the oars digging their way home.

Paddling with Dragonflies

Who is this restless couple,
this twisted pair, this light
iridescent heart
contorted abdomens
unwed confliction of wings
and short antennae,
their pulsing cadences
trying to straighten out
that which cannot be
straightened out,
but scorched instead
by the hard and the hot
deck of my old friend's
kayak, before she lifts them
with the cool blade of her
paddle and lowers them
down to the lily pad—lit,
to float in their room
not taken?

Cattails

in the
breeze
ten thousand
prairie thuribles

chained roots
unmoved
by hard
blows

sticks of incense
burn
on the
wind's breath

seeds
like ashes
blown
to dust

Empty Shell

The proud standing brass
now sits on my dresser,
long after the season,
waiting to be swept into memory:
an old cigar box
of numbed and fumbling fingers
on a snowy November morning,
220 grains grabbed from a fur-lined pocket,
and snapped into a metal clip,
like the unchosen cigarette
pushed back
to await its turn,
in the chamber for hours
and sometimes years,
in this country of few deer,
like a crabby old man
awaiting the children
who are playing ding-dong-ditch,
all this, for thirty seconds
of hot breath and a shot
which rips the cold out of the innocent
and finds daylight melting
in the snow,
ejected,
spent,
hollow in part,
with only the faint scent of success,
knowing there will be meat
for the winter,
and a proud brass shell
for my box.

Fritillaries

Sometimes late
at night,
in the dark square,
in the middle
of the frantic

checkmated
six-year-old's
slide down
into the frog
pond,

through the garter
snake's nest—
wet pants
caught slithering
up calves

burning
as I run up
the hill
towards home—
I think only of them:

the rescue,
an unchecked
flurry of orange
above the wind-
swept grasses.

To Aunt Sara

Is it proper etiquette doing eighty
heading to a funeral at the West Union Lutheran Church,
the road's dusty ash trailing like a giant Dionysian comet
billowing across the plains
exposing our tardiness to all the mourners,
to all those dressed in Angus black
who cannot see your grip on the wheel,
your punctilious guidance of the Subaru,
our vector of blind faith across the gravel,
your desperate pleading for me to hang on,
to remember the family's parting to allow us in line,
to remember one man's singing
holding us in a small country church
and the banging of the bell
as we opened the doors,
lending our ears to the wind
and our eyes to a swelling quiescence of prairie?

As proper as it is, I suppose, where I,
on a different vector now, thinking of you,
and the space between us defined
by a graying November day,
the red-dirt hue of the oaks covering the grave of the year,
the depression of sod huts and passing lives,
and desperate pleadings for you to hang on,
to remember us watching the rain
from a tar paper shed, to blind faith, gravel roads,
strong grips and, this morning,
the cold transparency of the first snow,
which has appeared, customarily,
bringing the soft prints of cottontails, retrievers,

children and grandchildren—wing prints of angels
to mix with the morning's smell
of wood smoke and *sejuk*—brightening all
with the formal joy of another season.

Letter of Incapacity

My old friend was a great outdoorsman;
he liked to fish the shallows for muskies
on glass-quiet evenings in early June.
He had a large capacity tackle box,
five drawers filled with topwater plugs
with names like *Zara Spook* and *Teasertail,*
and on the box's sides, four expandable racks
of *Bucktails, Buzzbaits,* and *Mr. Twisters,*
all of this convenient compartmentalized space
a preventative to those aggravating tangles,
the maddening open-bottomed jumbles
of food for fish thoughts.

I heard last June, from his youngest daughter,
that he drove his Yukon halfway to Minnesota
before he stopped, got out, and started walking
back home, on the freeway, in the cold rain,
and that the sheriff, who found him lost,
said that he was mumbling to himself
something about his open tackle box,
that he couldn't find the right lure,
that special hook-laden piece of painted balsa
that would bring the sulking monster
to the surface.

Early Modern Junco

A winter's gift to me:
you, the dark-eyed commoner,
winter's executioner of seeds,
hooded entertainer of kings,
under laden boughs of snow,
paused in your solemn deed,
a frozen prayer now
before the flash and peck
of your survival's needs,
before the wind whips
and applauding crystal showers
disrupt the scene,
and my soul has flown with thee.

Waiting for the Vet

Oil on canvas—Norman Rockwell

Turk, my uncle's Chesapeake,
never knew of Norman Rockwell's painting,
the tameness of the humbled waiting room,
the frozen pant of precocious breeds,
the sleepy consternations of their masters and mistresses
coyly suggesting that everything will be all right.

Humility came to Turk when he was kicked
down the basement by a previous owner
to wait in the darkness for nobody.
Later in life, he would enjoy a little more sunlight,
retrieving ducks, geese, the occasional farm cat,
and whole foxes across the fields and sloughs.
Everything turned out all right for Turk.

And still, I cannot help but wonder
as I sit here with my younger dog,
many humble lines removed from Turk,
just how tame we are eyeing the office cat
perched above us on the counter,
and how the painting and frame might change
with a simple retrieve from the slough of childhood.

Mice

Last winter we had a mouse problem,
nighttime murmurs in the basement walls
and the constant vigilance of Labradors
kept Grandma company during her sleepless
nights, a tale of widowhood and old age,
paused, if only for a moment, by the scribbles
behind the drywall; after she went back to Arizona,
we set traps, and the walls were quiet again.

Last night, the neighbor bachelor-farmer
plowed under his fallow field;
we could hear his tractor mutter
and smell the graves of plants, uprooted.
In the backyard, a mouse fell
from its perch, high upon the dried-up
seed pods of the purple iris—
fell into an empty five-gallon bucket.

The labs show it to me this morning,
bug-eyed and weary in the circular maze,
the whole of its tiny gray mass shivering,
trying to be still—like concrete.
With forecasts for storms, heavy rain,
narrowing furrows, and winter
visits fast approaching, I let the dogs
inside and turn the bucket on its side.

Chronic

North wind wild
in the shutters,
clattering blows
bring cold down
on summer's breath,
snuffed-out,
a hard foretelling:
the pain of aspen leaves,
seasonal blight,
circulations slowed,
skeleton grays,
brittle bandages
wound too tight
to heal

Last Missile

Last missile in 448th extracted from a site near Hannaford
Griggs County Sentinel-Courier, September 19th, 1997

A convoy of neighbors and landowners
gathered today to pay their respects
to the passing of missile number 740899.

I wonder if Milford Gronneberg
said goodbye from his pickup?
He died today at seventy-five,
had tilled this soil well before the Cold War.
Milford loved Model Ts, sports,
woodcarving, and his garden.

Milford would have laughed at the sight of this
seventy-thousand-pound extraction,
a heavy soul for such a place.
His flight, I am sure, was less complex:
no cables, transporter-erector vehicles,
two lieutenant colonels and a squadron commander.

To say nothing about where Milford started from—
in a hole at Eidfjord Cemetery near Walum,
no steel-reinforced concrete,
no ten-foot, barbed-wire fence—
just a stone and the dying
sound of a prairie church bell.

Milford found his own way
past the thistle and the North Dakota mud—
lifted quickly by his protector, the wind.

Hunting in October at 5 am

Standing in the folds of the northern plains,
it is dark—
quack quack chuckled
high-balled-up pinions-spinning
dark.
You know alone
the fear of stars
not shining.

But stand still,
your feet are stuck
in North Dakota mud
and a badger hole
awaits your next step,
to pull you back
when you feel yourself spinning
and lost.

Needlegrass, Bluestem, Foxtail Barley—
these prophets of the prairie
like straightened scripture
keep you chaste,
until the sun comes up
turns over the sky
and releases you
into the blue.

Migration

November's blizzard
bolts the door,

all motions immovable,
thoughts of progress stalled,

walled-off:

shelf ice:

the wing-shot Gadwall
stands on one leg

awaiting winter's
starved coyote.

Classifieds

For Sale:3-year-old purebred 'no papers' Brittany Spaniel,
excellent markings, great with kids,
shots current would be good hunting dog, $125 OBO;
9-foot church pew in good condition;
organ, bench, and music books, make an offer;
girls twin size bed with headboard and footboard,
wrought iron; 2 end tables, oak with glass.
                    Kulm Messenger, February 9th, 2000

Far beyond the township news
and the school board minutes
and the worries of a shrinking population,
are a few short lines,
ones to remember and hold close,
protecting them with waving
grains of memory—
these are the classified lines
which make me want to call my father,
like he too might call me.

"I made an offer," I tell him,
and we drive right over—
wife and child wretched and half-asleep
slipped from bed into an aging Ford Explorer—
off to Grandpa's house
where Grandma huddles,
her blue knit hat pulled over her ears,
holding a leashed Brittany pup,
her eyes lit by our headlights
like a child who has forgotten
the message on judgment day.

Away we go into the night
with a few hundred in cash, some gas, and high spirits,
passing by our usual spots,
the Clark County Forest, Alexandria,
the gateway to the northern plains,
and finally coming to Kulm, a small prairie town,
where we part with our money and load ourselves up
with an organ, benches, books, pews and beds,
and another fine-tempered, *no papers,* Brittany spaniel.

And as the sun crests the eastern plain,
someone will finally see us, making our final offer,
prayer books scattered
in the deepest furrows,
high on a prairie pass:
my wife and daughter asleep on an old twin bed,
I laid back on an unstable church pew
reading the etchings of canvasback,
my father, far off, out walking the dogs,
and Grandma, hat off, back straight,
arms and fingers extended,
playing Amazing Grace on the organ.

The First Day

My Spinozist Labrador is blowing
her shofar this morning,
a rubber chicken stuck between her paws.
She is not alone:
geese plod in the wheat stubble,
cranes stork their way across the bean field,
chickadees flit in the balsams
and I, here on the porch,
listen to it all through the rise
and fall of my breath.
We all sing this morning
We all praise the change in the wind
overnight, a change in the season,
a new time—
Barukh ata Adonai!
It is autumn.

Grandpa's Story

You will not find this in the hunter's log,
the way he comes to the kitchen,
his davening done,
holding two teal and a pintail
stripped of their regal colors,
blood dripping on the floor.
He seeks tools for the cleansing,
a can of Sterno, that singeing smell
from his childhood,
a pan of water to wash the insides out,
and a bottle of Royal Host Sherry
to splash upon the cutting board,
a toast to the embers of the season,
and a knife enough to sever legs and heads,
leaving one strong wing to identify
what species we have and who we are.

Diagnosis: Osteoporosis

During the first snow of November,
the little birch tree by the shore
flutters like a flock of goldfinches
among the brittle certainty of firs,
its fragile heart-shaped leaves
weep for last summer's spring,
but still cling, dance, sway
and shimmer at the hip
through the wet white veil.

A Hymn for Miley

After dinner, as mosquitos
hatch in back alder swamps
and begin their short lustful lives
traveling beyond the edges
of their still-water homes,
you trundle down to the edge of dusk's dock;
slow in your descent, your nails click and drag across
the aging slivered platform,
a gray warped springboard of time,
to stare down the minnows through cloudy-eyed
reflections, and to hear the loon cry
through evening's blue mist.

Here you wait for me, wait for me
to bring the rod and bucket
one more time, one more time to nip
and jump at bluegills and rock bass,
one more time for me, one more time
to miss your missteps,
your flailing ass-over-tea-kettle into water,
your shake-to-share the joy of it—
but with the splash and spray, the myth abates—
you didn't have twenty years to wait.
So, with your head bowed and ears perked, I leave you
as the evening swarm forces me inside,

and a minnow leaps through the sky.

Death of a Naturalist

It happened at an intersection
in the middle of almost nowhere
at the edge between the green
tamaracks and the wide open
above the flowering of muskeg...

At his shack, three days later,
a slow stream dissects the clearing,
a doe nudges her fawn to drink,
pale etchings of bear claws
weather the garage door closed,
a buck-horn helmet protrudes
under moss-laden eaves,
a calcium cradle of spring
robins' detritus, broken
now above a bustle
of Black-eyed Susans,
a limp dog chain draped
over an empty kennel,
a thistle feeder hanging
a half-day from empty,
and a flurry of birds,
Golden-Crowned Kinglets,
skyward.

Self-Quarantined

think of the aging brook trout
under a low-cut grassy bank
sheltered from the deadly glare
of midafternoon
ignoring the false
hook-laden offerings
from midstream
in favor of the fragile caddis
born of hammocked incubation
held by translucent wings
about to lose its grip on the blade
just above home

Epitaph for a Duck Hunter

Of all methods of duck shooting,
that known as pass shooting
is perhaps the most difficult
and the most sportsmanlike.

American Duck Shooting,
George Bird Grinnell

Bury me on Woodhouse Pass,
where the north wind can blow
flurries on my belly,
and the canvasback can etch my stone.

Put me down where I can feel
the thump-thump of the hunters' soles
and hear their shots and cries
in a never-ending season.

Let the sharps boom out my passing
from this low valley,
where two lakes converging
find me born.

Let the cranes be my angels
and carry my spirit
into the prairie light,
that I may continue my hunting.

Bury me on Woodhouse Pass,
where I can see my children play,
let me witness their celebration
at the dawning of a new day.

About the Author

John Fritzell lives in Appleton, WI, with his wife and two very part-time hunting dogs. A graduate of Grinnell College and employed in the financial services industry, John was short-listed in *Tiny Seed Literary Journal's* Annual Chapbook Contest and a finalist for the *North Dakota State University Press'* Poets of the Plains & Prairies (POPP) Chapbook Awards. John is a member of *The Mill—a place for writers* and the *Wisconsin Fellowship of Poets (WFOP)*.

Made in the USA
Columbia, SC
20 July 2021